Fathers Feel too

Fathers Feel too

a book for men by men
on coping with the death of a baby

Andrew Don

SANDS
STILLBIRTH AND NEONATAL
DEATH SOCIETY

Published by Bosun-Publications
The Ferry Point
Ferry Lane
Shepperton on Thames
TW17 9LQ

Tel: 01932 242436

First published in Great Britain in 2005
by Bosun-Publications on behalf of
SANDS (Stillbirth and Neonatal Death Society)
28 Portland Place
London W1B 1LY

Tel: 020 7436 7940
Helpline: 020 7436 5881
Email: support@uk-sands.org
Website: www.uk-sands.org

ISBN: 0-9546932-3-X

Fathers Feel too. Copyright © 2005 Andrew Don

A CIP catalogue record for this book is available from the British Library.

Typeset in 12pt Minion
Printed in England by
The Cromwell Press Ltd

Book design and production by
FW Barter ARCA
Bosun-Publications
Email: fbarter@bosun-press.demon.co.uk

Cover design by Chris Hoskins
Cover photograph by FW Barter

CONTENTS

Page

Dedicated to Lara Jean Don, whose death
gave two other children a chance of life,
to my wife Liz and to my courageous daughters with love.
To all the brave men who contributed to this book and for the
souls of all the children who missed their chance of life…
this is for you with love.

Foreword

On September 20th 1996, ironically my birthday, my partner Julia gave birth to our fifth child, Grace. She was full term but stillborn. Everything about her was perfect, from her tiny finger nails to her familiar pointed chin. My most consistent genetic legacy to my children has been a distinctively shaped chin and Grace was no exception.

As Julia suffered, giving birth to our dead child, we could hear a family through paper-thin walls, celebrating the birth of a healthy baby. After Grace was born, Julia stood, desolate, holding her baby. Her grief was overwhelming, tangible and immediate. A mother who had lost her child. I, the father, watched from 10ft away. I watched and wondered what my role was, what I should feel, how I would grieve, where I fitted in.

Every father who has felt the dislocation, confusion and sadness of losing a baby should read Andrew Don's important book. *Fathers Feel too* gives us permission to grieve. It reminds society that for every grief stricken mother, there is a father struggling to articulate his own despair.

But Andrew Don's greatest achievement lies in the book's ultimate optimism. By helping fathers to identify and express their grief, he is laying down the foundations of future hope and healing.

David Haig
August 2005

My story

Lara Jean Don, a five-month-old foetus, died some time between June 3 and 4 1997.

Lara Jean was not just any foetus. She was my little girl…my hope, my future, my light.

For five months I'd sung *Baby Face* and told my corniest jokes, head pressed against Liz's womb.

I was your regular one-man cabaret.

Now, as I stared at the ultrasound, she looked almost big enough to say, "Hello world, here I come."

She was beautiful.

She was dead.

A horrible wail emitted from the woman whose belly was freshly wet with ultrasound gel. It didn't sound human. It came from a deep place that even I, her husband, had never witnessed before.

It was like a Middle Eastern funeral and a wolves' wake rolled into one. I took one look at her stricken face and the grief was too much for me. I roared and head-butted the wall. "Not again, not again," I screamed over and over.

Both our reactions were instinctual, animalistic. When you lose a baby, the most base instincts emerge. We become who we really are, just another part of the animal kingdom, stripped of societal pretences.

I had never been one to hold back my emotions, never the stereotypical macho male. I always thought that a good thing. It made me compassionate, sensitive and a good listener.

But now it felt like my little girl had just been ripped out of my own imaginary womb.

There would be no other children. We had known that this would be our last chance after month after month of fertility treatment: the highs, the lows, the crushing disappointments.

Our dreams of parenthood had started to evaporate when the hospital admitted Liz to the ward at 12 weeks with high blood pressure.

Her "care" there was like something out of *Fawlty Towers* except we were not laughing.

They lost her notes, faxes disappeared, basic medical checks were either forgotten about or undertaken haphazardly.

The idea was that she should stay in bed and relax. But the shenanigans that went on just made her blood pressure shoot up further. The night before our baby died, they put her next to a mentally ill woman who was screaming abusively all night.

The concern was that Liz might develop pre-eclampsia, a dangerous condition that can only be alleviated by delivering the baby. Pre-eclampsia can be fatal for both mother and baby and the consultant thought keeping Liz in hospital would help prevent its onset.

Events came to a head on June 3 when a midwife administered a different blood pressure drug to the one prescribed.

The subsequent failure that night to monitor Liz led to a life-threatening surge in blood pressure culminating in pre-eclampsia and the loss of our baby.

When Liz had told the registrar her stomach hurt, he had given her Fibrogel for constipation. When she said she could not see properly - blurry vision is one of the signs of pre-eclampsia - he suggested she might have got aromatherapy oil in her eyes and recommended drops.

I could not believe that staff who were supposed to be monitoring Liz specifically for the purpose of preventing the onset of pre-eclampsia, failed to recognise the symptoms when they manifested.

When a few weeks after Lara Jean died, a condolence letter arrived from the consultant addressed solely to Mrs Don, I flipped.

What was I – a non-person? Lara Jean was my baby, too. I'd read the books and seen the movie. I was prepared for fully-fledged fatherhood. I had signed up for the full deal. Count me in, I'd announced to the universe.

Even the extended family did not have a clue. My sister's in-laws wrote a letter of commiseration to Liz. What did they think my role was in all this – merely a detached penis that did the dastardly deed?

For five months I had dreamed of what it would be like to be Lara Jean's dad.

Now, in cold, impersonal letters, the hospital, and even some family, did not acknowledge me or my grief.

My mother died of cancer when I was 14. This was at least as bad and brought up the old emotions of loss.

I needed revenge. I got a solicitor and for nearly a year I took the steps necessary to take the hospital to court for negligence. I was grief-stricken, angry and desperate for someone to pay.

Liz had had fertility problems ever since we got married. We'd been through IVF and every possible route we could to try to have a baby. All you men who have been down to the IVF clinic month after month, been tested for all sorts of nasties such as chlamydia in the most horrible invasive ways and seen your wife or partner go through procedure after procedure, know exactly what I am talking about.

Liz hates injections and I was terrified of giving them. But I thought she was going through so much that it would be an ultimate act of love for me, as her husband, to give her the Profasi injections that were required before embarking on a course of IVF. I cannot ever begin to explain how I felt giving my wife those injections. My stomach lurched. But I felt I owed it to her to personally administer them because she was going through so much. I tried to be gentle and precise, but the fear of air bubbles meant it took all my concentration to keep my hands from trembling – not good when I had a syringe in my grasp.

Now, into her mid-40s, we knew this was it - we would never be parents. We always thought we would make such a caring and loving mum and dad. Parenthood, to us, was not something that we wanted because it was the expected thing. To us, the idea of parenthood was vocational, something we both felt was meant for us.

After we lost Lara Jean, I developed sores around my mouth. I knew their cause was psychosomatic. The anger, the pain and the grief that twisted me inside were showing themselves to the world in physical form. When I heard other people had had babies, jealousy consumed me.

I wrote to then health secretary Frank Dobson with a dossier of all the things that went wrong at the hospital. He did not reply.

After about a year, I had to drop the case because of the financial risk involved - I did not qualify for legal aid and did not have legal insurance at the time - and because, after getting a veiled apology from the head of the NHS trust, I decided it was time to let go and live again.

I had to move on.

Several books helped me to make the first steps. I read everything by Paulo Coelho – *The Alchemist,* in particular, had a massive effect on me. I also re-read books by Rabbi Harold Kushner, such as *When Bad Things Happen to Good People.* Gary Zukav's *Seat of the Soul* and Neale Donald Walsh's, *Conversations with God* series which drastically changed my attitude.

A new spiritual dimension gradually found its way into my life, albeit not in a religious sense – conventional religion always sucked as far as I was concerned. I discovered I was able to channel healing and began training as a spiritualist healer. Every day, I tried to improve myself.

I was on holiday with Liz in Malaysia a couple of years later when I brought up the subject of adoption. On July 7 2001, we officially adopted two sisters.

I got to be a dad in the end. Maybe not in the way I had always thought but these two children are our children, nonetheless, and we love them deeply.

Fathering is not about physically creating a baby. It is about parenting. And just because a child is not of your flesh does not make them any less deserving of your love. With adoption, if you make the child your child, then they are yours just as surely as if they had come from your sperm.

Being a dad is an attitude – not a condition.

I will miss Lara Jean until my dying day. But something good came out of her death – two other children got the mum and dad that they so badly needed.

So why this book?

I was researching an article for *The Times* about men

and childloss in May 2002 when I realised how there was nothing in the bookshops totally dedicated to men that spoke directly to their hearts, in simple, readable language.

I was able to express my emotions – I screamed, head-butted walls and cried more tears than Alice in Wonderland but, on researching my article for *The Times,* I discovered that most men feel under pressure to keep their emotions in check.

Dads don't count. They're the stiff-upper lip cavemen of yesteryear whose involvement in childbirth and pregnancy are limited to the initial sex act and the obligatory cigar nine months later as far as society is concerned and it seems to make little difference wherever in the world you come from.

Ruth Bender Atik, director of The Miscarriage Association, in the UK, told me: "Our experience is that men are often excluded full stop in pregnancy loss. The expectation of the man is that he is strong, silent and sup-portive."

I realised then and there that there was a need for a something men could anonymously pick up from the bookshops or order off the internet, a book that showed how greatly many men suffer when they lose a baby whether pre-term, at birth, or the first few years of life.

I got in touch by e-mail with men all over the world ask-ing them to send me their stories. The only qualification for inclusion was that there should be a light at the end of the tunnel. It was difficult. Those, for whom the experience was still too fresh expressed support for what I was doing but could not imagine ever coming out the other side. These are the men for whom this book is so important. Many others, who had come out the other side, felt awkward about articulating their experience.

For those who went through the painful process of sending me their stories, I am eternally grateful.

For many men pregnancy is not something that happens to their wife or partner. It happens to the two of them. It is the couple who are pregnant. It is a joint deal. Martin Kunz, who describes his wife Samantha's caesarean in Martin's story, says: "*We* had an emergency caesarean…"

This is a book about men who care, about how men grieve and how they bravely struggle to deal with their pain against the constraints society places on them.

This is a book to empower men and give them hope, for those that love them and to help the medical profession understand what may come as a surprise to some but, yes, fathers feel, too!

Life does go on after the loss of a baby.

April 7th 2003

In memory of Lara Jean Don

I

Lara Jean - our loved, lost child
We hurt, we bleed
Where only a month ago
You grew within us,
Where once we heard your thumping heart
It pumps no more
And we cry:
We cry for our child
We'll never know,
Our little girl
With tight brown curls
And large brown eyes
Just like her mother's;
We cry for our child
Who should have discovered
The joy of living,
The joy of love,
Her first ride at the fair,
Now nothing's there -
Just pain where once you grew.
And I the father suffer
Like I were a mother
For I loved you child

Like I loved no other.
I sit here by your grandmother's grave
Surrounded by the stones of numerous lives
Who have suffered throughout time
And I want to join them
There in the earth
So I feel no more pain
So I feel no more hurt.
How proud she should have been.
The same wind blows
The same trees quiver
As they did when cancer stole her
So much time has passed since then...
How I have grown.
My mother, my child
You are both lost
We hurt, we bleed
From the wound where you should be.

Lara Jean, our loved, lost child
You are much loved
You are much missed.

Andrew Don

Mark's story

Our first child, Timothy, was born in 1989.

He arrived seven weeks early and spent the first month of his life in the Special Care Baby Unit (SCBU) at Crawley Hospital, West Sussex.

He developed into a healthy little boy.

It was not long before we wanted another child and over the next few years Julie, my wife, had two miscarriages. Each brought with it sadness and grief although we always knew that we had Timothy and we were grateful for him.

In early 1993, when Julie fell pregnant again the usual excitement and hope for the future came tinged with anxiety - would there be another miscarriage?

Previous miscarriages had happened before the 12th or 13th week of pregnancy so when we got through to about 15 weeks we felt more hopeful.

After lunch on Saturday June 12 1993 when Julie was in her 26th week of pregnancy, she started to get pains in her stomach. We wondered if these were Braxton- Hicks practice contractions or just indigestion. But the pain intensified and by mid-afternoon it became clear they were contractions.

Our doctor called for an ambulance and Emma was born within twenty minutes of our arrival at hospital. The normal pleasures that accompany most full-term births were absent.

I suppose I was just relieved that Julie was okay and I was assuming the worst for Emma. It didn't occur to me that Emma could survive at all so I was surprised when the consultant told us it could go either way.

He warned us that even if things did work out well, Emma would be in hospital for a long time and it would be a fight every step of the way.

Emma only weighed about two pounds. Her skin was so thin you could nearly see through it. Her lungs were not developed enough for her to breathe for herself so a ventilator did the job for her. She was unable to maintain her own body temperature and she had to be kept in an incubator. There was no milk from a mother's breast and she had to make do with the cold comfort of a drip.

Julie was well enough to come home after a few days and we started to settle into a routine of visits and phone calls that turned into a six-month emotional rollercoaster ride.

There were periods of great excitement and also fear during this six months as Emma's condition took a step forward or back. I also had the added responsibility of supporting Julie and my only son, Timothy.

Our lives revolved around the hospital. We got to know the SCBU staff really well and we lost contact with our friends.

Crawley Community Church gave us a lot of help. Another couple in the church had previously given birth to a premature baby whom they had lost. Their understanding meant a great deal to me although I hoped our story would have a different ending.

My work colleagues also gave me a lot of support. My job already allowed for flexibility but my manager's understanding was exceptional and gave me the freedom to be where I felt it was most important to be at any particular time. It was a real challenge trying to work with everything else going on.

I kept a diary during Emma's life. On Wednesday July 14 1993, I wrote:

We prayed for a breakthrough and we got it. When we got to the unit we were told that she had put some weight on. She was now 2lb 5ozs. This was wonderful news. Julie also was allowed a cuddle; this pepped her up even more.

This was all great but then at 7.30 this morning we had a phone call from Brenda, the sister in charge of the SCBU, who was elated. Emma had dislodged the tube that was down her nose and throat the night before and the doctor had decided to leave her without a tube for a while and just use a head box. Breakthroughs on two fronts - weight and lungs, Yippee!

The next day I wrote: *Yesterday morning Brenda from the unit phoned to tell us Emma had come off the ventilator. Brenda was thrilled and so were we. All day I was impatient for my visit to the hospital. Would Emma still be off the ventilator or not? When we finally got to the hospital we were so pleased to see there was still no ventilator. This was the first time we had seen our baby's face without the breathing tube in her nose or mouth. This was indeed a high spot.*

On Friday July 16 I wrote: *This has been a good week. By yesterday evening Emma had been off the ventilator for nearly two days. This was better than we had hoped for; even Caroline, the specialist midwife who had special responsibility for Emma and us, was surprised at her progress. We are aware that if she gets another chest infection she will have to go back on the ventilator. Last night Julie was able to cuddle Emma for the first time without the ventilator tube. Her face looks so different without the tube and like a good little Kendal she seems to like being cuddled, one of our better family traits!*

But on July 21 1993, a Wednesday morning, things took a turn for the worst. The entry in my diary reads: *When we arrived at the hospital on Monday evening we were barred from entry to the unit. June, a member of the SCBU's staff, and another nurse stood in the doorway and asked us to go down to the waiting room because Emma was having the breathing tube reconnected. We waited there for forty minutes. Eventually we were allowed in to see her. It was distressing to see her with a tube stuffed down her throat again.*

The consultant explained that in the end she was exhausted and was having too many apnoea attacks. Emma looked poorly, her skin was pale and she had dark rings under her eyes. Staff planned to give her some extra blood later. They suspected she had an infection and put her back on antibiotics.

I needed to know everything that was happening to Emma. I must have driven the SCBU staff mad with my phone calls asking how she was. I wanted to know every detail: ventilator pressure, oxygen saturation, type of medication, level of medication, plans for change in treatment. A vague, "she's doing OK," or "not so good" left room for my imagination to run riot.

The more I could understand the medical detail then the better I felt able to deal with circumstances as they arose.

If my phone rang I would jump. Usually, a phone call from the hospital would bring bad news.

In the last month before Emma died it became clear that her condition was getting worse; her lungs were in a terrible state. We realised that earlier progress had probably been because of the heavy dosage of drugs that could not be administered long term.

Most of us can live quite happily with an oxygen concentration of about 21%. Emma was barely coping despite being surrounded by pure oxygen. By the middle of November, five months after her birth, we realised that short of a miracle, it was unlikely Emma was going to survive. We were resigned to agreeing that should she stop breathing, the staff were not to try and resuscitate her.

A phone call from the hospital woke us early one Monday morning. Emma's condition had become much worse and we should come in as soon as possible. Miraculously, she rallied on our arrival, evidently insistent she was not leaving yet. For all her small size and ill health, this little girl was a fighter.

We got through the next week living day to day, but the next Saturday, we got an urgent call from the hospital. Her condition had taken a turn for the worse.

There in Crawley Hospital's SCBU on a Saturday evening in early December 1993 Julia and I cuddled Emma and showed her how much we loved her. Emma was barely conscious but we believe she enjoyed these last hours of affection.

Finally after several hours, her breathing became more and more shallow and then it stopped. We looked at each other, then Emma breathed again. It seems silly now but we laughed!

A few minutes later Emma took her last breath.

I remember the morning after Emma died so clearly. I awoke and after barely a moment realised that she was gone. I sobbed and sobbed.

It was hard coming to terms with the fact that she had gone. As a Christian, I was confident that she was in a much better place and that I would meet her again some day when my time on this earth had come to an end.

But I wanted her alive…now.

The days passed after the funeral and we had to come to terms with our loss and adapt to life without our daughter.

The odd thing was I missed going to the hospital. We had spent so much of our time there during Emma's life. Now, if we visited the SCBU, although we were welcomed, we did not belong anymore - a most strange experience - like walking past a house you used to live in.

Initially Julie and I were sure that after such a tragedy we would never get upset over the small frustrations of life again. We then spent the next few months getting incredibly upset, impatient and generally miserable over the smallest incidents or misunderstandings. That is, I guess, one of the ways that grief had its effect.

As the weeks turned into months, we started to move forward. This did not come easily but I believe that my relationship with God gave me purpose and direction. I did not then - and still do not know why we went through all that we did, although I know of many people who have endured much worse.

In the first weeks and months after Emma's death, Julie and I were certain that we would never want any more children. We could not face going through all that pain again. Then as the months turned into a year or so - and to our own surprise - we found that our view had changed.

Julie became pregnant again bringing with it a tide of mixed emotions and the familiar anxiety-tinged excitement. The doctors were not taking any chances. Julie had to endure a weekly injection, which kept her awake practically all night every Friday after it had been administered. She also had to undergo a surgical procedure to try and prevent the baby arriving early and she was confined to bed rest for long periods.

Our new baby Esther managed to cling to the womb until the 35th week of pregnancy. At only five days old we were able to bring her home – no more of the endless weeks of hospital visits.

Esther was big compared with our first two children. She weighed more than 5lbs. Today, she is seven years old - bright, strong, happy, healthy and beautiful.

I like to think I have matured through the whole experience. I hope I am more sympathetic. I confess that my eyes moisten a lot more easily than they did before.

Life does go on but I do not believe that time in itself heals although we do grow a protective layer over our emotional wounds. I believe that God has helped me through this whole period even though I do not understand any of the whys and wherefores.

Like many others I now regard the people that surround me as even more important than I did before.

Mark Kendal,
systems engineer,
England

In memory of Lara Jean Don

II

From Nakatchafushi

Cool wind washes kisses on wings of summer's rays
Skims over sandy carpets, glides in on clouds of wishes
Past palms and thatched eaves bathing
Like hungry egrets thrusting
Into the throbbing coldness
Of a dull, spiked ache.

Hot air like magic fingers knead tortured crippled muscles
Enchanted sunbeams try to batter hatches locked with hurt
Wisdom's spirit rides the surf
Arm in arm with Mother Earth
Upon an ethereal blanket glowing
Shrouding all within its reach.

Nakatchafushi - a song in whispers
Nakatchafushi - a song of pain
Nakatchafushi - my lost, dead child
Nakatchafushi - with you I lay.

Andrew Don

Graham's story

My name is Graham and I am 34 years old.

I have two beautiful sons, aged 18 months and three years for whom I would lay down my life.

I try hard not to impose my own aspirations on them or my hang-ups, but when they are older, I would like them to understand that not only do I love them for themselves but also for the two older brothers or sisters we never had the chance to meet, know or love.

As I write this, I can see that in some respects the suffering was really the beginning of me becoming a man - one who would be able to sustain the kind of relationship that three years of fatherhood have taught me are not only necessary to survive as a passably sane parent but also a prerequisite to raising resourceful, compassionate and happy kids.

I am of the post-AIDS generation for whom safe sex was part of my consciousness. I consider myself a relatively intelligent, well-read man with strong working class origins - neither 'New Man' nor 'Lad'.

I spent my early twenties and late adolescence trying to get on with enjoying life and developing a career in a fairly prescribed fashion.

As a child I never had any significant family male role models - brought up by a single parent, estate-raised, comprehensively uneducated and in receipt of what the state has the audacity to describe as benefits.

If you ever get the opportunity to listen to *Up The Junction* by Squeeze or even better, *The River* by Bruce

Springsteen, you will grasp my fears in terms of my life in relation to parenthood at that time.

My view towards both marriage and having children in my early twenties was that they were activities that others engaged in, although I have always liked children and had engaged in community youth work as a volunteer.

I experienced a major shift in my life when I met the woman who became my wife. In some respects our courtship was the classic summer romance that never ended. We had mutual friends, worked in the same profession and both shared a big interest in Guinness. We still laugh when we wonder how many couples' special song is Talking Heads' *Psycho Killer*.

We began to live together within a month of meeting or rather, as my wife would put it, she had a key and used it on the way out in the morning and when she got home every evening, much to her papa's chagrin.

We were married in April 1995. I cannot ever really recall making any concrete decisions about when to have children although an imperceptible shift had happened; enough to turn an 'if' into a 'when', no doubt with the help of my wife who is from a large family.

I had never really understood the concept of trying for a baby. Sex never seemed the chore that trying implied to me at that time and by August 1996 we thought our attempts must have been successful following a weekend in Amsterdam.

The strip on the pregnancy testing kit turned a positive blue to whoops of delight and discussion as to whether our test might represent the 0.00001% inaccuracy described on the back of the box.

Apart from being happy, carried along by the moment, I did not really know how I felt. I was not particularly nervous. It felt right; I felt ready and we were financially and emotionally secure. It seemed like a natural progression for us.

Some friends and family made discreet comments about it being early days. Their motivation may have been protective but I did not need to hear that kind of stuff.

However, at the same time, I exclaimed quiet disbelief at people buying loads of kit and decorating the nursery if a period was a few days late - not quite but you get the idea.

My wife did not smoke although I did at the time - in the garden - and she was a teetotal, nutritionally sound vegetarian receiving regular midwifery input.

One day she noticed a small spot of blood in her knickers - no pain, no warning, nothing. We contacted our midwife who referred us to our local early pregnancy assessment clinic where we sat in a waiting room with several other people.

We were frightened and expecting the worst.

The sonographer who gave us an ultrasound said she could not detect a heartbeat and that the doctor would want to see us.

Whether the news had not hit home or she was very brave Sarah did not cry much at all. I did not know what to do, say or feel. I felt unable or unprepared to cry and was mostly concerned for Sarah.

We spoke to a genuinely sympathetic male doctor who could answer every question we posed except the only one I wanted to have an answer to - WHY?

We went home only to look at each other, cry, cuddle and take phone calls.

At the time it did not really occur to me this was happening to me as well. Not only did the actual miscarriage not seem like anything I had ever seen on television or in the movies but it was also something that affected women and not men.

We returned to hospital the following day to share a ward with women terminating unwanted pregnancies so that the remnants of our child could be removed from my wife's womb. I walked her into the operating theatre and sat waiting for her to come out. It was the most frightening experience of my adult life to date.

I did not know what to do.

Sarah bled constantly following the "straight forward little procedure" for 11 weeks. The day before Christmas Eve a large piece of tissue also appeared.

The final remains of our baby gone - flushed away.

Life carried on, albeit a little strained relationship-wise, and our house slowly stopped looking like a branch of Interflora. I developed a hatred of homespun philosophy and statistics as to how common miscarriage is and worked hard on developing an interest in Stella Artois.

Shopping expeditions became a nightmare for my wife: pregnant women, newborns, and clothes. Although I tried to understand her pain, I did become impatient at times. I also wished I had someone asking how I was and that I had been able to articulate the things going on inside me.

Men are as much the victims of miscarriage as women. All of a sudden everyone came out of the woodwork to say they, too, had had one which seemed to lessen my right to feel such great pain.

I was unable to give a name to my feelings let alone feel in a position to articulate them to anyone whatever their capacity. A supportive GP prescribed anti-depressants which I didn't think helped. I wasn't depressed. I was a bereaved Englishman.

I did not feel that the counselling on offer would have met my needs – or, at least, I was not prepared to believe it. I am an atheist so I did not even get the chance to blame God.

Life went on. It was not as good as before but it slowly improved.

And in August 1997 we were expecting again.

We were both beginning to believe that things were going to go well when in the 13th week of the pregnancy Sarah, who was feeling unwell, was advised to attend the Early Pregnancy Assessment Clinic.

It was another miscarriage.

My closest male friend John was with me while Sarah was in the operating theatre. He is not the most emotionally open person I know, but when I told him how cursed I felt he gave me what I can only describe as the kind of hug only fathers can give their sons.

I will be forever indebted to him. For that moment he could not change the pain but he carried some of it for just long enough when I could not.

The aftermath of our second miscarriage was the biggest test of our relationship. For a time we lived separate lives together, bound by our past but not by our possible futures.

For the first time in our lives, having a child became a mission. Sex became a chore for me, timing everything, and foreplay an irrelevance. I would joke that I was only wanted for my sperm - not quite a sex object but, in a way, that is how I felt.

Sarah had joined the Miscarriage Association. She had also become a telephone contact for women who had experienced miscarriage – a role I think that helped her to heal herself.

The work the Miscarriage Association does is outstanding but as a man I somehow felt, at best, on the periphery. I would read an occasional account penned by a man but did not feel empathy particularly.

For whatever reasons, conception was not happening and we were referred to our local reproductive medicine clinic. The only conclusion was that my wife and I were of different genders and devoid of any known genetic disorders.

In our relationship we had never shied away from expressing our emotions in no uncertain terms (think Richard Burton and Elizabeth Taylor). I did not appreciate the rough treatment of my genitalia in order to rule out any "structural" problems and I will be eternally grateful to Caprice for her assistance in (part) filling that test tube, if only in my imagination.

At our next appointment Sarah's otherwise clockwork cycle was late. She was pregnant... again. What should have been fantastic news filled me with sheer terror. I did not know if I could go through this again.

And I was worried about the impact of any problems on Sarah's health and our relationship.

Our third pregnancy was marked by further anxiety when an early scan detected a possible kidney abnormality which can indicate Down's Syndrome. The pregnancy continued with a watchful eye kept on kidney development. On August 27 1999, following a labour lasting over seventeen hours, our baby became very distressed in the womb.

Sarah had to have an emergency caesarean section before our first son Jordan made his entrance into the world. After four years of not being able to deal with how I was feeling, all of a sudden I was presented with a whole new set of emotions.

I will not even attempt to describe these because I do not think however rich a language is it could even adequately convey the reality – the rest of you blokes will know what I mean.

I do not remember sleeping much so I cannot imagine how we made love but within nine months we were pregnant again. Our second son, Joshua, made his entrance in February 2001 after a relatively uneventful pregnancy.

When the midwife invites you to cut the umbilical cord she never warns you that you will get spattered in blood – I thought I had developed freckles and would not have washed for a week if I had not succumbed to pressure.

What happened happened. I will never forget our losses but I do not dwell on them. It does not work for me that way. I have even needed to check dates with Sarah so I can write this story.

My children have enabled me to have a mission in life: to try, be persistent, understanding and the best parent I can be by acting as the role model for my sons that I wish I had had when I was growing up.

I no longer smoke, I exercise regularly, I am less stressed and I have developed a balance between my work and home life.

My experiences of loss have made me realise what a good choice I made in my mate. They have made a major contribution to my becoming a man capable of being a good enough parent and partner. I am much more able to deal with whatever life throws at me.

Loss, however bad, need not be the end.

Graham Paul
England
(Graham Paul and all the names in Graham's story
have been changed at the request of the writer)

In memory of Lara Jean Don

III

From Kuramathi

Rush...
Hush...
Silver fingers roar
Then diminuendo
Gracefully tickle
The shore

Yesterday beneath a ceiling of palms
On hammocks we swung
The inky darkness above
Casting shadows
Between the spidery limbs
Of an unknown plant
And the ground
I fell into the drunken stupor
Of a snapshot moment
Tranquillity etched on my heart.

Today we leave a fairy isle
A hybrid creation of man and God
Not as nature intended
But beautiful still
Where man has made good.

And I fear the world of deadlines and pace
That stunts spiritual growth
Fear the return to pain
Of a child lost
To medical ineptitude
I pray to a God for the strength to cope
And wonder if he hears...

Yet I see him in the silver fingers that roar
Then diminuendo
As they gracefully tickle
The shore.

Andrew Don

Chris's story

We were so happy when we found out Anne was pregnant. We hugged and kissed and danced around the house.

And, indeed, everything was fine at first.

When we went to the hospital together for Anne's first scan there was something almost magical about seeing our baby move, the little heart beating, the right number of arms and legs.

And we discussed how reassured we felt by the scan on the journey home.

But during the spring of 1990 Anne's blood pressure started rising and she was retaining fluid. The doctor advised she should take it easy but I insisted she took a week off work after reading how dangerous pre-eclampsia could be, a potentially fatal condition for both mother and baby which can only be resolved by delivery.

Then as March came to a close, we worried our baby had not been moving as much as before. Anne's blood pressure was high and the doctor, with his usual bland "oh-I'm-sure-everything-will-be-fine," attitude sent us to the hospital to be scanned and monitored.

The midwife's initial response was that the baby was not the 31 weeks we said it was. Babies of women with high blood pressure tend to be smaller than their age would suggest. She kept saying the baby was only about 25 weeks. Anne got upset when the scanner operator asked: "And what have you been doing," as if she had done something wrong.

When we went back up to the labour ward we were told

that the high blood pressure had prevented our baby from growing normally and he had only developed to an equivalent age of about 26-28 weeks instead of the 31 weeks we knew him to be.

The hospital did not want to deliver because it did not have the facilities to look after such a small baby. We discussed transferring her to another hospital, in southwest London, but the plan changed when Anne went back on the monitor.

Suddenly the trace dropped right down and stayed low, unlike on previous occasions when it had reassuringly risen again.

There was no time to transfer Anne. The doctor said she must have an emergency caesarean there and then.

"If we don't then the baby might die," he said.

Within minutes, Anne was prepped and in the theatre. That was the worst moment for me, I think, seeing Anne wheeled in, frightened and confused, while I was left outside, alone, unable to help.

My son was delivered just before 6pm and taken upstairs to the special care baby unit (SCBU). I went to see him minutes later. He was not much bigger than my hand.

All around me machines were bleeping and buzzing. As I touched my son, a wave of emotion swept over me. I could not control it, the tears and despair. This was not how it was supposed to be. This sort of thing happened to other people, people who did not look after themselves, people who didn't care.

Not us!

The nurse and I took Polaroid photographs before I went back to see Anne, who looked pale and fragile. When Anne came round, she asked how our baby was.

"We have a son," I said.

"He's going to die," she cried, over and over.

I tried to convince her that everything was all right even though the same thoughts kept jumping into my head.

I returned to the SCBU not long after because Anne was sleepy. The nurses explained to me what the equipment did and encouraged me to stroke our boy.

Just as I was about to leave, he opened one eye and looked straight at me. My heart turned over. This single response gave me great faith that everything would be all right.

The consultant explained they could not look after him where he was for more than a few hours. He was transferred to a specialist children's hospital that night.

I went home but I couldn't sleep. I read and re-read all the baby books I had to try and find out everything I could. I needed to try and find a reason why this had happened.

The next morning I found Anne in buoyant spirits. We looked at the photographs and decided that I should go to London to see our son whom we decided to call Drew Alexander. It was the only boy's name that we had both agreed on.

Drew was derived from a German name meaning strength so that settled it and I went and registered his birth - for me, an act of faith.

I was overcome with emotion on the train to London and as I walked to the hospital. When I thought of Drew I could feel my tears well up and my stomach churn.

I walked down the corridor to the neonatal unit. I still see that long, long corridor today in my dreams.

Then there he was, tiny, naked, strapped up with wires and tubes, looking so vulnerable. I cracked - I just could not stop crying.

When I had calmed down, Tracy, the nurse who was looking after Drew, explained all the machines and alarms to me again. She told me Drew was doing well and that a doctor would come and talk to me soon. After the doctor had talked to me they had to draw off some of Drew's blood to check the oxygenation level.

The first time they did it I wanted to tell the doctor to be more careful but taking blood from a vein the size of a strand of cotton is difficult even when you only need a couple of drops.

I took more photographs and then went to get them developed. The neonatal unit was hot - the babies are all naked to enable the nurses and doctors to care for them easily. I felt drained after a couple of hours.

Later, I went back and I just sat holding Drew's hand and stroking him. He opened his eyes a few more times but he seemed very tired. I started to get used to the hissing rhythm of the ventilator and the buzzing of alarms going off.

I left and caught the train home. I sat and looked at the photos. It seemed unreal that the rest of the world was carrying on its daily business not knowing about Drew. I wanted someone to see the photographs and say something to me but no one did.

I took the photographs in to show Anne. I think it was a bit of a shock to her because they showed how small he actually was. I did my best to cheer her up but she was upset that she had not had a chance to see Drew before he was transferred.

Later, I went home and started phoning friends and relatives to tell them what had happened. People react in different ways but there was always the same comment, "Oh they can do marvels these days." I suppose they did not know what else to say.

The next few days blurred together as a routine was established: visit Anne in the morning, visit Drew in the afternoon, back to see Anne in the evening then home to phone round the day's report.

I borrowed a video camera and took some film of Drew. Anne still had not seen him after five days in hospital so although it upset her when she watched the tape, it kept her in touch with our son.

Eventually, they let Anne out for the day. We drove up to London and got to the hospital. Anne found everything very difficult. I had started to get used to how Drew looked but it was all new for her. The staff got Drew out of the cot still attached to all his wires and tubes but, at last, Anne was able to hold him. It was a great moment.

The most difficult thing with a premature baby is the swings that occur from day to day. One day everything looks promising and you start to have hope for the future. The next day something goes wrong and despair sets in. The doctors always give you the worst diagnosis to every little problem. This keeps your hopes in check but it can cause unnecessary worries.

Drew was now getting most of his nutrition through a long line, a tiny tube which entered his leg and finished near his heart. He was being given total parental nutrition (TPN), which was made up every day and contained all the proteins, fats and vitamins he needed. They would analyse his blood and vary the amounts required for the next day. Drew's weight varied a fair bit. He weighed 1lb 13ozs when he was born and after an initial drop, his weight gradually climbed until after four weeks he was up to almost 3lbs.

The care in the neonatal unit was intrusive: no sooner had they finished one procedure than they seemed to be starting another. There was not a lot we could do but we were encouraged to clean him and oil his skin. The babies get very dry under the heaters and ultra-violet lights. Sundays were best because not so much was done and there was more quiet time for us with him.

Drew's stomach became distended and tender. Many suggestions were given but no real answers. But after four weeks, it looked as if Drew was doing well and he was breathing on his own in a head box which provides an oxygen rich atmosphere.

So it was all the more a shock when he suddenly got pneumonia. His health deteriorated rapidly and we were warned to expect the worst.

He rallied and seemed to get a little better but with such small babies one problem can trigger off several others.

On April 30 when I got to the hospital they told me they had rung Anne and she was on her way. They felt we needed to be there.

Anne arrived with my sister, Melanie, who had given her a lift. We were told they did not expect him to last a lot longer. Had we thought about getting our parents to come and see him? We had always resisted allowing visitors to come to the hospital. Apart from anything else, we knew what a shock it would be to see such a small baby with all the equipment and wires attached. Was this the way we wanted people to remember him?

We decided to call my parents and gave them the choice. They came to see him, of course. My mum was crying and I think my dad wanted to as well but couldn't.

We went for a walk after their visit. Again, I experienced a sense of unreality. People were going about their normal lives while my baby son was dying.

When we went back to the hospital, the doctors were trying to do everything they could think of but ultimately they had to tell us what I think we knew already - Drew was dying.

They asked if they could just keep him comfortable and we agreed. It was a long night. Anne and I stayed in a room at the end of that long corridor and cuddled together on a narrow bed crying and dozing.

At about 4am, I walked down again to see how he was. I could see straight away that all the monitors and levels were very low but he seemed peaceful enough. I sat and stroked his hand for a while. I tried to tell him how much I loved him, how important he was to us, how he would always be special to me and how proud I was of him.

I returned to Anne and then at about 5.30am, the nurse came to fetch us. Drew was fading fast. We decided we wanted to hold him without all the wires and tubes. Carefully, they disconnected everything and that is exactly what we did.

He took a couple of more breaths and at 6am on May 1st he died in Anne's arms.

We held him for a long time and then we took him back to the room we had stayed in. All the nurses and doctors came to see us and tell us how sorry they were. One of the nurses said: "We're not supposed to cry, but we do."

I held him up to the window. He had never been able to really see the world. Tracy, the nurse who was looking after him that first day, came to look after us.

There were various formalities to go through. I had to

register his death in London within the next seven days. I decided that I would do it there and then. The hospital arranged for a car to take me to the Registrar. I waited about 30 minutes for the car to arrive and when the driver said: "It's lovely weather today." I snapped back, "Yes you don't expect people to die on a nice day," which wasn't very fair of me I suppose.

At the registry office, all I could think of was that I was sorry for the poor girl who had to deal with me and what a rotten job it must be.

When I got back to the hospital, Anne and Tracy had given Drew a bath and dressed him. Anne said she felt that at last she had been able to do something for him. I really regretted not being there with her and eventually we had to leave and go home.

It was a strange day - so many different emotions. We rang all our close friends and family and arranged the funeral.

Peter, the hospital chaplain, had offered to take the service and he suggested having a burial, something I was unsure about. Anne wanted to so I agreed. We went to the cemetery and the superintendent there was really helpful. He showed us the children's section and said we could pick a plot almost wherever we liked. We chose a spot at the top of the hill. I was worried that we would have to take the next plot in line but it wasn't like that.

Peter encouraged us to think carefully about the service we wanted and, in his words, he would "keep the God stuff to a minimum". We used some poems we had found, *The Wind* by AA Milne and another, *A Lily of the Day* by Ben Johnson. We both wrote Drew a letter which we put in the coffin. It was a good way of saying things that maybe would not make sense if you said them out loud.

We went to order the flowers and had an unfortunate experience with the girl in the florists. We wanted to have white lilies but she could not understand that I would not pick an arrangement from the book. I wanted something special for Drew. I wanted someone to make an extra effort for my son. Anne got upset with me for making a fuss but fortunately the manager understood what I meant.

When the day for the funeral came, the weather was wonderful - sunny and dry - something that was important to us because we wanted to have the service outside.

I cut some flowers from the garden, the funeral director came to pick us up and I carried Drew into the house for a few moments. He had never come home with us properly. I carried the tiny white coffin to the grave. The hole seemed huge.

Lots of friends and family attended the service and nurses from the hospital and work colleagues. After everything was over I felt strangely vague interspersed with bursts of intense sadness. This continued for at least the next two years.

It seemed strange that I couldn't even visit the hospital to sit and talk to Drew, or stroke his hand. Things that other people got worked up about suddenly seemed very unimportant. The feelings don't really go away but they get easier to deal with.

On July 20 1991 Anne gave birth to Elinor.
Anne had problems with pre-eclampsia again and ended up spending about five weeks in hospital.

I held Elinor for the first time - she wriggled in my arms, so strong and full of life - so different from the last baby I had held.

I fell in love with her then and it still feels the same every day I see her.

But when I held her up to look out of a window I always thought of Drew and wondered what might have been.

Chris Hoskins
Surrey
England

Chris and Anne went on to have another daughter, Jessica, who was born in 1993.

In memory of Lara Jean Don

IV

Lara Jean
You should have been born
This week
I should have held you in my arms
Smoked my fat cigar
Raised you in the air and cried:
"I name you Lara Jean"
Like Kunta Kinte...
I should have been the delirious father
Who Cheshire cat-like
Beamed with imbecilic grin
Like the first time lover
Who pats every child's head
To whom even a skunk is fragrant.

This morning our cousin had a little girl
You would have played with her
He holds her proud
As I should have held you
And the sadness drowns me.

It's Zero Day
And I don't know
Where to go from here...

Andrew Don

Gideon's story

Having children was easy, I thought.

I already had two teenage children from a previous relationship.

They were intelligent, healthy and beautiful and I came to see this as the norm.

But a year-and-a-half ago my new partner Julia had an ectopic pregnancy. I remember her wide-eyed delight when she became pregnant and how this changed suddenly to worry when she developed pains in her abdomen.

They discovered the problem, took her into hospital the same day and operated to remove her left Fallopian tube and the tiny foetus. When she was recovering from the general anaesthetic she looked grey and old, and I remember feeling a pang of grief – or possibly another emotion. Whatever it was, it seemed to be more compassion for Julia than about the baby itself.

Over the next few weeks Julia surfaced slowly as if from a deep sleep. She is emotionally very expressive. Her wound was real and it was clear to me that she needed time to mend. Her body had been damaged but also her opinion of herself as a woman seemed precarious. My concern was much more for Julia than about the loss of the child.

Julia felt the baby had been a girl. We gave her a name, Emily, and talked about planting a rose bush to remember her by.

A few months later Julia was pregnant again and although the carefree joy of her first pregnancy was not there this time, the weight of grief of her loss seemed to have passed. At 21 weeks into the pregnancy we went to the hospital together for a scan. Seeing the baby on the screen brought home to me that I was going to have another child. It was a boy. This was no longer a small swelling in Julia's abdomen but a real baby and I felt a surge of pride and hope.

The radiographer seemed to be having some trouble getting good images of the baby's heart and she asked if we would mind moving to a different room where there was a better machine. In the other room a woman in a white coat joined our radiographer and they started to discuss the images on the screen in low voices.

This went on until I found myself asking if something was wrong. I held Julia's hand. After some hesitation the radiographer explained that there seemed to be a problem with the left side of the baby's heart. She wanted the cardiac specialist to give Julia another scan to find out more. Julia started to cry silently.

The cardiac specialist explained in a level voice about the flow of blood into and out of the baby's heart. It was clear that the left side of the heart was not developing properly. Later in her office she explained to us that our baby appeared to have one of the most serious heart defects there is. Twenty years ago he would have died within a few days of birth but more recently a series of operations had been developed that increased the chance of survival to about 25%.

Babies like this were known as "blue babies" because of the difficulty that children brought up with such conditions have getting enough oxygen into their blood.

Our son could expect to spend the first few months of his life in an incubator, would probably be able to go to

school but would spend a lot of time in hospital throughout his life – and it was impossible to guess at his life
expectancy because the operation had only been available
for 18 years.

The specialist gave us a booklet with case histories about
people who had brought up children with similar conditions and those who had chosen to have a termination
instead. That was the choice available to us now. It was
Friday; we arranged to discuss our decision the following
Monday if we had managed to reach one.

That weekend was one of the most awful experiences of
my life. When I was younger my failures and inadequacies
led me to depression and sometimes made me think of sui-
cide. But there was always a romantic element to the experience. It was as if I had kept part of myself detached to be
able to comment on and lament my position for posterity.
Once I even walked across Clifton suspension bridge to
find the best position to jump from – and noted it down in
my diary.

That weekend I did not care or even think about what
people thought of me and my decision about our baby.

My image in the face of the world had become unimportant. My focus this time was on the baby. We spent the
weekend in the flat reading the case studies and talking out
all of the arguments we could think of, back and forth. We
talked for an hour or so, paused for half an hour and talked
again. We held each other and wept much of the time.

On Monday, we saw the specialist again and told her
that we had decided to have a termination. When explain-
ing the reasons for our decision I remember the feeling of
guilt for the first time. I was the one who had pressed Julia
for this decision and although she now agreed with me, my

feeling was that I carried the main responsibility for what would happen next.

Then came more horrible information about the termination process. Julia would have to give birth to the baby because of the length of the gestation. They would also have to do what was euphemistically described as "stopping the baby's heart" two days before birth so that he wouldn't be born alive, because if he had been born breathing the doctors would have been obliged by law to try to keep him alive.

My feelings were of frustration, powerlessness and anger mixed with a lot of compassion for Julia and, of course, more guilt. Through the intense emotion of this meeting I remember the gratitude I felt to the specialist for not judging us for our decision one way or the other.

The fact was that in many ways I felt that my decision to abort the baby was wrong. On balance, the opposite decision seemed to be even worse, but I know that if she had shown it, the specialist's disapproval would have been very hard to bear – because at some level I would have felt such disapproval to be right.

While waiting for the day of the birth, we decided to give our baby a name. He would be called Thomas. Giving him a name seemed to make him much more real to me and brought tears to my eyes again.

Finally we went to the hospital, Julia was induced and gave birth to a tiny baby some hours later. We took it in turns to hold him and I wept more than I have ever done since I was a child. He looked perfect, with tiny hands and feet and I imagined how he would have moved if he had lived.

Pure sadness engulfed me.

I don't remember how long we took – it was probably a day and a half – but when we were ready, we left Thomas in his little cot and went home. The nurses were wonderful and had encouraged us to stay with him as long as we wanted. They had taken two photographs of him and made prints of his hands and feet, and Julia put these away in a drawer with her diary.

Julia needed time to recover and I left her to her thoughts as much as I could. We went to the Isles of Scilly for a few restful days. Her depression seemed much deeper this time, however, and after a few weeks, I started to worry that this had become a way of punishing herself for what we had done. I felt I needed to be strong for Julia, to show her that I still had beliefs and that I wanted life to go on but I was confused.

The people around us were mostly supportive but they often seemed to need to make sense of our experience on our behalf. Hearing from a friend that I would have more lovely children, that it was for the best, that Thomas would have had a difficult life in and out of hospital; all of these things seemed true but had a hollow ring to them.

Later I realised that I had been trying to understand what had happened. I had been searching for a meaning for Thomas's death, and the explanations that my friends offered never quite rang true. In reality, there seemed to be no reason for what had happened and no redeeming features to the experience. It was just horrible and black and one of the experiences of life that we all hope to avoid.

I ran my own business from home and in my emotional confusion I plunged myself into my work. Eventually I decided that I needed to do something to bring Julia back into the world of the living and pushed her aggressively back to her own work again. She held that against me for some time but it did bring her out of her depression and it seems now to have been the right thing to do.

Just after Thomas's birth we had talked about having a funeral. Julia and I are both atheists so this was not for religious reasons but to mark his death properly and close the experience. We reminded each other every few weeks that we had agreed to have a funeral and "must do something about it" but this brought looks of dread into Julia's eyes and it took me almost six months until I was ready to arrange it.

We contacted an inter-denominational minister who helped us to design a service to express how we felt about our child. We invited six close friends and relations and arranged the funeral, almost by chance, on the shortest day of the year, the winter solstice.

The funeral really did help me to let go of the uncertainty and confusion I had felt. The months of chaos in my mind before I felt able to arrange the funeral seemed now to have been necessary and I was glad that I had not given in to the urge to force order into my thoughts and to come up with a rigid rationalisation of what had happened. Even though I had never seen him alive, I knew as I carried his little white coffin into the chapel and afterwards to the grave that I had loved our little boy and that was the most important thing.

As I read during the service about my experience of his birth and my uncertainty about whether I had done the right thing, my feelings felt clear. They were of sadness and loss; the taint of guilt seemed to have gone. It felt as if I had done my best, even if that was not very good. We all went home to the flat, drank some champagne and the day seemed to be lighter again.

Ten months have now passed since Thomas's funeral and Julia and I have a new baby, born September 24 2002. He is beautiful and I find myself utterly fascinated by him. While he is asleep, feeding at his mother's breast or gazing about with awe, I find myself staring at him, barely aware of time passing. It seems so extraordinary to see this tiny creature that has grown from Julia and me into this relaxed, healthy new being. I am not surprised that he is healthy – expectations do not seem so important to me now – but I am certainly relieved and very, very happy.

Gideon Mitchell
London

In memory of Lara Jean Don

V

Lara Jean
My child that should have been
Born today -
You who were in the hospital's care
Killed by a drug
Mistakenly administered.

Like a trapeze artist
Her blood pressure soared
My baby dead
My wife at death's door.

Not far away
Lies a mother and baby
A little girl -
Your cousin
Whose face I cannot bear to see
A reminder of what might have been
The world that you will never see
A child that will not know our love

Lara Jean
I cry for you
Lara Jean
Let the pain flee far
A child born of special love

We longed for you
We tried so hard.

The brandy does not numb my hurt
The ultrasound flickers before my eyes
My fully-formed daughter dead before me
Our howling echoes
Then silence
Too hurt to cry aloud
Like when a door crushes your fingers
And you can't make a sound.

I remember smashing my head against the wall...

The machine turned off
Clinically
With our hope.

Andrew Don

Tony's Story

Nobody could prepare me for the horrors that were about to unfold when we had our second child.

Only the day before, I had put the final touches to the new kitchen and playroom we had built.

On the day of the birth, Louise woke up early to tell me she had not had the expected number of kicks. We went to hospital to be on the safe side. She went into labour after an interminable wait.

I phoned my father-in-law and arranged for my son, Joseph, to be picked up knowing that when he returned he would have a brother or sister.

The first indication that something was wrong was when the nurse could not pick up a heartbeat through the ultrasound placed on my wife's belly. So they swapped the machine. Still nothing.

The white coats in the room cast anxious looks. They called for a different kind of monitor with an internal probe that they attached to the baby's head. I looked at the white coats. They knew what was happening but they were too afraid to say.

The specialist became more frantic as he swapped the probe for yet another.

Still no news.

Louise, all this time, was going through labour, digging her nails into my hand while I gave her gas to keep her calm. How many more people could they fit into this pretty pink room that was getting darker by the second?

At last they made the decision to deliver by emergency caesarean. We were rushed into a lift. Everybody was shouting at me to give my wife gas. The last thing I remember before I was shepherded into the room where my son was born two years earlier was the sound of Louise screaming: "Save my baby, save my baby."

What a difference it was now, sitting alone in the corner of this room, so empty and dark.

What seemed like an eternity passed before the midwife came in. I saw tears in her eyes. "What's wrong?" I asked.

She said my little angel had died. I asked about my wife but nobody would answer me. I wondered if she had died as well.

I cried. Never have I cried so much.

When the porters wheeled in a drugged Louise I had to tell this wonderful, beautiful woman that we had lost our baby. She did not seem to really understand. The midwife asked if I wanted to hold our baby.   My breath caught in my chest.

Are you mad, I thought? How can I hold a dead baby? I had never experienced death like this. I could not cope with this. I could not hold my baby.

I did not know how much I would regret that decision. For years after, I felt that my arms were extended but holding nothing, leaving a deep emptiness.

Louise drifted in and out of consciousness for two days and when she did come round she went into shock. The hospital staff were attentive, making Louise as comfortable as possible and gave us photos of our little girl, "Bethany". She was so perfect, so pretty, and I remember thinking how big she was.

Throughout this time I had to try and keep it together

for my little boy and walked around the hospital with him for hours.

When we got home, Louise was still recovering from her caesarean so I had to arrange the funeral. I think the worst part was choosing a dress for Bethany to be cremated in. What do I know about baby's clothes?

Then came the funeral and organising the headstone. What do you write for the baby who did not have the chance of life?

I carried Bethany in her little white coffin and placed her ashes in her resting place on the coldest day I have ever known.

For months after, Louise would go to bed early while I drank whisky. We really did not say too much until Louise was ready to try for another baby - I suppose to fill the hole in her life. I was not too comfortable with this but went along with it. Our first attempt ended in a miscarriage.

At this point I decided to remove as much of this period of my life from my mind and left the company I worked for. I think most people were probably fed up with looking at my miserable face. Not only did I start a better, well paid job but I also decided to change my outlook on life and I made a conscious decision to enjoy myself.

This job was perfect…entertaining on expenses, which meant going out lunchtimes and sometimes continuing through the night, getting home at a ridiculous time.

I think Louise was more interested in getting pregnant and she was able to cope without me now that I had got us over the technicalities of dealing with death, organising the funeral and caring for her during her grief.

I now felt surplus to requirements.

I became a Jeckyl and Hyde…when I drank I felt fantastic,

enjoying every second. When I went home and sobered up, I wanted to die. When Louise confronted me in my drunken stupor, all I could do was cry at the loss of my Bethany. I was destroying everything. Even when I found out that Louise was pregnant again I could not stop. What's the point when you think it is going to happen again?

By the time Eloise was born, healthy in every way, it was too late. I was on the road to ruin...I went to the doctor after I got a pain in my thumb.

The doctor was mortified at the amount of drink I was consuming and suggested a blood test, taken by a lovely lady who knew my wife. How embarrassing was that!.

"Mr Dobbyn, most of your blood is alcohol...I have booked you in to see a mental specialist," he told me when my results came back a week later.

I felt bad before. Now the doctor was telling me I was mentally imbalanced. Thirty-three years old, alcoholic and mad.

I have always been immaculately dressed and felt slightly out of place and when the specialist called me in she gave a little bit of a surprised look.

I told her about my Bethany and some of the things that were going on at home and about my drinking.

She considered me for about a minute...I thought here it comes we are going to commit you...

"Mr Dobbyn, you are grieving and tired that's all." She gave me are some bereavement counselling numbers instructing me to call them and take a few days off.

You cannot believe my relief. I got home called the numbers and spoke to Maurice and Joan Lacey at Compassionate Friends who arranged to meet us at a meeting for bereaved parents. Louise found it too distressing and did not return for another year.

I went to see a hypnotist on my days off. George got me to focus on not relying on the booze. It cost me a fortune but I could afford it and it was worth every penny.

He told me he thought I had the potential to be a spiritual healer. I was initially baffled. He arranged a meeting in London where I was interviewed along with 80 others, knowing that only eight would be chosen.

I did not think I had a chance so I forgot all about it. I was shocked when I got a call from the Greater World Christian Spiritualist Association. I was still working for my company and went to the spiritual meetings in the evenings.

After completing my course at the Greater World, I spent two years working with my teacher George as his apprentice. Now I am a fully qualified healer giving healing to those that ask for it.

When I give up my career in the City I plan to become a full time healer and set up a sanctuary for those who are suffering.

My mind became more balanced and when I began healing, the drinking almost stopped. I decide that I wanted to do more for bereaved parents and became the assistant at Compassionate Friends to Maurice and Joan.

I became the team leader for the monthly meetings offering counselling for grieving parents. At last I had the opportunity to give something back…my life was changing for the better. The crowning moment was when I received an award for voluntary services, nominated by the parents that I had helped.

None of this would have been possible without my belief in God. When I had hit rock bottom, it seemed God was there. Now I know that through my faith, I can overcome any obstacle and help others.

My story is dedicated to my Bethany. I know that every thing I do will be for her memory. To waste my life would render her loss worthless.

Tony Dobbyn
Senior IT manager
Essex
England

I cried on the death of Diana

I don't like royals
I don't adulate stars
I was not a sheep
Who fell at her feet

Then I heard Dolly Parton
Sing I will always love you
Saw the video of her so alive
And I cried

But not for her.

Andrew Don
September 1st 1997

63

Dwayne's story

Danny died one week after our wedding of Sudden Infants Death Syndrome (SIDS) – he was six weeks old.

Pamela and I had met in high school. One thing led to another and she got pregnant before we married. It might not have been the smartest thing we had ever done but we loved each other and so we got married.

But the joy I should have experienced at being a father was short-lived.

I still don't know how I survived the initial shock. I tried to deal with my grief by totally focusing on the future and almost completely ignoring the past.

That was the way I felt I needed to deal with it but it was not fair on my wife. Nor was it fair to Danny who deserved to be remembered.

I took to drinking which helped me numb the pain for many years even though we had another son but the pain of Danny remained always just below the surface.

When our third son, Kenneth, came, there was a problem during labour. The doctors discovered he was in distress and had to deliver him by emergency caesarean. He had a collapsed lung and some other problems.

He spent two weeks in the intensive care unit and I found this was almost unbearable after I had experienced losing a child. He did survive, however, albeit with mild cerebral palsy, communication problems and some other motor control skill difficulties.

Rather unexpectedly, we later had a girl, Bethann. We were living in a bad neighbourhood because I was still working in a fastener factory for appalling pay.

I drank daily to drown the pain of Danny and my shame at being unable to provide my family with a better life.

Pamela needed me to help her deal with her grief but she felt she could not talk to me. It hurt our marriage and we went through several periods of separation.

Today, after all out pain, I can tell you there is a light at the end of the tunnel, at least there is for me. We got back together and found ways to talk to each other without screaming and hurting each other's feelings. We also got involved with a SIDS support group.

I took up karate four years ago during one of our separations in an attempt to do something constructive with my time. As I got into it more, I found drinking was hurting my reflexes and I slowly gave up alcohol. I have found that having total and complete self-control is a greater feeling than the buzz from drinking.

I now hold a black belt. I have been promoted at work where I am a cold forming engineer and department foreman. I have found that I truly love what I do for a living even though it is a hard and demanding job.

It might be a cliché but it is so true that time will always keep moving on. You'll have good times and you'll have bad times. Throughout, there is always hope for the future which is a blank page that has yet to be written. You can do anything with it you like. As a martial artist, I believe you can do anything you set your mind to.

A lot of men deal with grief the way I did, I think. What I should have done was look to my wonderful wife for the strength I needed to survive and to help her get through this.

I still hurt sometimes for my son but that's okay. Just like an old injury, the scar will always be there and hurt sometimes. Now, with my kids entering teenage years, I fear that we are entering a new era of turmoil, but this time I hope we can deal with whatever comes, together.

Dwayne Dearing
Warminster,
Pa. USA

Space

Space -
Furtively furrowing
Trenches of thought
Through furlongs of field

Wait
For sparrows to drop
Creativity's seeds
For germination

Anticipate
The roots take hold
Pray for rain
Pray for rain....

5am start
8.30 deadline
Supermarket trolleys
Fluorescent light
Ovulation
Write out an invoice
IVF jab

Make love to a test tube
Banana fritters
Are all well and tasty
But time fritters away
Ice-cream for some space -

Furtively furrows
Space
Stop
It will wait for tomorrow
Slow
Pace
It will all end in sorrow

Andrew Don

Richard's story

My heart aches for my missing daughter like the amputee whose missing limb hurts.

Camille Rayana, eight pounds, 21 inches long, perfectly formed with a cute "button" nose, was stillborn August 17th 2000 at John C Lincoln Hospital, in Phoenix, Arizona. I got to wash and dress her. I got to hold her. I got to kiss and photograph her. And I got to cry for her.

In time, we gave her up to the nurses. We had decided in the midst of our grief to donate Camille's heart so that her valves could save another child's life. Just the belief that a piece of her may be living on in this world made it a more tolerable place for me.

We held the memorial service at the Salvation Army Adult Rehabilitation Centre in downtown Phoenix, a locale familiar to my wife Sharon. We refused professional help and crafted the service in our own way, calling on officers whom we knew to participate, and interspersing scripture with song. Not traditional hymns but more worldly compositions. *Tears In Heaven,* by Eric Clapton, and Rogers & Hammerstein's *You'll Never Walk Alone* from *Carousel,* sung by my wife Sharon's sister.

A sonogram in January had confirmed that Sharon's pregnancy would be a normal one. Two years earlier she had an ectopic pregnancy that resulted in a ruptured fallopian tube and her obstetrician wanted to be certain that the foetus was not in her other tube.

Amniocentesis was strongly recommended because Sharon was older than 39 and I was 60. Our baby was genetically perfect, we were told. After much persuasion, our doctor said we were having a daughter.

Like every parent-to-be, what we wanted more than anything was a "healthy baby". But, if we could have chosen, we would have selected a girl. Sharon and I each had our own reasons for wanting a daughter - me because I wanted a baby who would grow up to love her daddy more than anything in the world, a baby who would cuddle on my lap and look at me with adoring eyes and likely never come home with a frog in her pocket.

Sharon had been apprehensive. Early in the pregnancy I said all the right words, but she sensed the spark was not there. She told me later that she wasn't sure I really looked forward to being a parent.

The truth was I was afraid, not of being a parent but of not being a parent. As she began to "show" and the baby began to move, I found myself asking her - sometimes hourly - if the baby was moving. I was so afraid of disappointment that I dared not invest too much hope and desire into a future that I had set into motion, but over which I had absolutely no control.

As the weeks passed and Sharon reached weight levels she had never known before, I dared allow myself to visualize being a father. Some time about month six, we began the ritual assembly, getting the nest ready. We bought the crib, a changing table, dressers and a rocker in which Sharon could sit and breast-feed Camille.

We now had a baby "in the oven", the nest was feathered, and Sharon was glowing with good health, an opinion shared by all who saw her. Even strangers in the market would comment she was glowing. She was also growing. Her gait went from that typical of a slender 120lb 5ft 7ins woman - who was once known for her "chicken legs" - to a woman of substance.

In the back of my mind was my brother's loss of a child to leukaemia. Andy was two when diagnosed and five when he died. I don't know what is worse, to go quickly or slowly. Death is death, slow or fast, infant or toddler, pre-teen or retiree. I am 60 but I am still my mother's child. She was 90 recently. She still gives me advice - eat slowly, don't talk with food in your mouth, try to exercise more - and would grieve like she did when she lost a son 62 years ago at age two if something were to happen to me today.

Children are not supposed to die before their parents. When a parent dies we lose a piece of our past but when a child dies we lose a piece of our future.

Shortly after losing Camille I was driving home on the Squaw Peak and out of nowhere I started to cry big time. I was torn between pulling off at an exit and getting home as quickly as I could but I pulled off.

I was recalling holding Camille in the hospital and kissing her sweet lips. I smiled as I thought of her. Her beautiful face, the perfect nose, and, oh, those lips. Suddenly I had a vision of her spirit flowing from her open mouth into mine as I kissed her. It was as if I were an observer standing in that room, as if I were slowly recalling a dream upon awakening. Her spirit left her limp body and flowed into mine. How else can I explain that I find myself writing with ease and a fluidity that I never had before.

I am certain that Camille is guiding me. She is with me. She is in me. We are together. She is my resident angel. I thought of her name and kept repeating it over and over as I neared home. It has taken on an aura of beauty and grace and sounds prayerful to my ear - my Camille.

I had trouble sleeping although I cannot blame Camille's death entirely for this. You see, I was expecting two babies this year, Camille and Colter Close. Colter is a 55-lot townhouse development on which I had staked my reputation and in which I have invested most of my capital.

Joanne Cacciatore – founder of Mothers in Sympathy and Support (MISS - www.misschildren.org/) came into our life two days after Camille's death. Like Sharon, she had a stillborn daughter.

Joanne forged her anger and grief into a worldwide organization, to come to the rescue of women everywhere who suffer such an unfathomable loss. In the overwhelming majority of still-born babies, autopsies confirm the death was for no discernable medical reason.

To the state, life exists for the living. For the rest we have devised body bags - zip 'em up and put 'em on ice, and tell us where to send the remains. That is what stillborn babies are to the state - remains. But not to the mother who carried that baby. And not to the father, who watched every kick and wiggle, all the while trying to imagine if it would have his nose. Or her mother's eyes. Or grow up to be president.

Not to me.

My daughter was not "remains". She is my daughter, now and forever. Sharon would tell me how she would turn in the womb in my direction when she heard my voice. Not alive? She was every bit as alive as an accident victim on life support. An umbilical cord is nature's ventilator. And a whole lot more. She was flesh of our flesh and to say she was never born is to deny our very own existence.

In the past 29 years I have been married three times, most recently to Sharon, Camille's mother, since Valentine's

Day 1996. I have earned and given away in divorce settlements more money than most people make in a lifetime. At the time of Camille's death I was in the thick of earning my next nest egg, this time for the love of my life and our precious daughter, my very first child and soon to be my proudest accomplishment.

The hardest part of being self-employed is the fact there is no boss. No one to set schedules, order priorities, list tasks to be accomplished. And in my case there are no partners. I have Sharon but it is not the same as having someone else in the business.

The other aspect of self-employment that is hard – especially for me at this time – is the loneliness. It is the second most common reason self-employed people give for going back to regular employment.

Many a time I would sit and a profound sense of sadness would descend upon me. A fortnight ago life was so rich and full of promise. At the age of 60 I was to become a father for the first time. Not a son to carry on the family name – which never mattered to me – but a daughter I could cuddle and love and prop upon my knee. I saw myself teaching her the computer before she could talk.

Labour Day Weekend 2000 and we spent it hiding behind drawn shades.

My mother had been the first to cradle Camille in her arms after I gave her up for others to hold. Imagine the pathos of seeing a 90-year-old woman holding her first grand daughter and kissing her still lips. "Why do I live and she have to die?" It is the question we all ask. There is no answer. God is not in the barter business. Instead we have to cherish our memories of that brief moment and try to find a reason to go on.

With no other children – just the two of us in our household – we had no distractions or other responsibilities to divert attention from our overwhelming sense of emptiness. Yes, there was my work, but that could not fill my empty heart. Usually we took turns encouraging each other but on one occasion we both hit bottom at the same time.

Sharon went into Camille's room. I had put the bassinette, stroller, swing and assorted baby paraphernalia from around the house in this one room before Sharon came home from the hospital. For the time being, Camille's ashes were there too, along with the outfit she was photographed in at the hospital. This outfit was carefully laid out in her crib as though she had just slipped out of them to take a stroll and would be back any minute.

Next to the rocker where Sharon sat, she picked up Camille's Memorial Book containing all the hundreds of e-mails we received from MISS members around the world. She had already read every one of them as they arrived in the days following Camille's death. The flow diminished to a trickle and we were once again alone with our thoughts.

It was important to Sharon that the room be straightened and the clutter carefully put away in the closets. That done, she was able to sit down in the rocker and picking up a bag of items from the service, withdrew two photos from that awful day. One showed Camille with her arms crossed and her fingers encircling a rose that our friend Jim had obtained from the gift shop in the hospital. It was the photo we displayed at her memorial service.

The other was of Sharon and me with Camille cradled in her arms. In the picture, Sharon looked at me and I looked past the camera lens into eternity. Camille's eyes were closed.

"Are these the only pictures?" she asked. In fact I had taken about 20 pictures, though many of them were variations of the same pose. A few were taken of me kissing Camille but I don't remember who took them. I presumed Jim. I left Sharon in her rocker crying and I went to my computer and selected 5 to print and show her.

For a long time she said nothing. She just looked at the pictures, turning the page from time to time so as to get a different perspective. Then she broke the silence. "Can you print a copy of this one for my wallet?" she asked, pointing to the photo of me kissing Camille on her lips. The kiss when her soul merged with mine as I believed. I promised I would and left Sharon alone to sort through her memories. She joined me in our bedroom about 10 minutes later. She settled in with *Chicken Soup for a Mother's Soul* intending to read but quickly fell asleep instead. I followed her in a few minutes.

Sharon doesn't talk about her feelings easily; she is a very private person. I, on the other hand, can't be stopped. There's no right or wrong. It is how each of us copes with crisis. But this night we both spoke and the topic was the emptiness we felt.

For Sharon, it was both an emotional and physical emptiness. Just weeks ago she was full of child and now there was none. Not in her belly; not in our bed. Her breasts, engorged with milk in the days following delivery, went back to normal size. And her belly, which she proudly displayed and allowed others to feel throughout nine months, visibly retreated as days passed. Her body erased every trace of Camille's brief existence.

We asked at the hospital about drugs to dry up Sharon's

milk but were told side effects had caused health care providers to avoid this therapy. We were told about massages, warm showers, and time as the principal means of dealing with mothers who lose their babies.

I took to the internet. I found lots of answers but an intriguing one kept showing up in odd places like chat rooms and newsgroups. "Tell your wife to put cabbage leaves in her bra and change them frequently as they wilt."

Sharon had just gone through a devastating loss and all I could find to offer her to ease her breast pain were cabbage leaves. I wrote to the La Leche League whose website is replete with helpful information for nursing mums but has little for mothers who have no baby to nurse. They came back the next day with the same recommendation, as did a friend in Sacramento. I put a lid on my scepticism and headed for Safeway. Red or green? I forgot to ask. Since green is the more common cabbage, I chose two heads and brought them home.

I had told Sharon the cabbage story before I left for the store and her attitude was why not try it. It couldn't hurt. Upon my return I tried to inject some humour into the situation for the first time. "The produce section was out of cabbage so I got a pint of coleslaw from the deli instead."

It was good to see her smile. Maybe we would survive this terrible loss.

It was time to get on with the business of living.

I decided to go back to work, in earnest. More importantly, I would get out of the office. Everything at work went like clockwork. People who I needed to speak to about specific projects happened to be in the right place at the right time. So many coincidences happened that day that I found it hard to believe that someone was not looking out for me.

For three months after Camille died I stared at walls during which time I put together her memorial website.

I have since founded the National Stillbirth Society, the first and only advocacy website for stillbirth on the internet.

My experience has been that life really does go on.

Richard K. Olsen,
Executive Director
The National Stillbirth Society
Phoenix AZ.

In memory of Lara Jean Don

Lara Jean

VI

The intercom buzzed
A voice said it was Mel.
She had the baby with her
I was prepared for that;
Lara Jean's cousin
Same sex
Same age
Same month of birth.
I looked at Jodie
And Jodie looked at me
And for a moment
She was Lara Jean.
Here, nine months on
I looked at a child
And saw what ours would have been
Should have been.
I cradled her in my arms
And she looked at me
I looked at her.
As if for a second
She understood
Just a second;
The next…uncomprehending.

I looked at proud dad
And happy mum
And the emptiness hit me again
Where you had died
And for just a moment
I understood why people stole new born babies
From devastated mothers who wailing
Plead for their return on News at Ten,
Those baby-snatchers who previously
Made me spit at the screen -
"LARA JEAN
LARA JEAN"

April's coming
And once again
I understand why it's
The cruellest month
How well I know Eliot's rain
That stirs dull roots
The mix of memory with desire
The forgetful snow that fed
A little life with dried tubers.

Through winter the crocus bulbs pushed through the earth
Mild days encouraged them to flower early
A hopeful omen thought I of fertility and birth
But April's near
And we are sterile.

Andrew Don

Martin's story

We still can hardly believe that after 10 years of heartache, shattered dreams and loss of hope that we have everything we ever dreamed of today.

We lost five babies between November 1992 and September 2000.

One of them, Claudia, was born prematurely and made it to six weeks.

I remember so vividly how we dressed her and put a little rose in her basket. We kept expecting her to awake and we did not want to let her go.

Samantha and I had previously suffered two miscarriages and we had given birth to a daughter, Rebecca, who had died in the womb.

I am not sure if words can ever adequately describe the feelings and emotions I experienced.

I still struggle to come to terms with the loss of our children. To be honest, I do not know how I am ever supposed to "get over it". We are all told we *will* get over it.

I never contemplated not having my own family. I come from a large brood and have two brothers and three sisters - most with children. So the first time my wife fell pregnant we had no notion that anything could go wrong.

The professionals tried to comfort us with statistics when we lost our first child. "It happens to one in three," they told us. You are still young and you can try again."

They showed little interest in trying to understand what had happened. Perhaps some people will find it difficult to understand how totally distraught I was over losing a baby I had not known - especially as I am a man.

It is not just about the death of a baby, which is immensely difficult in itself because you are mourning someone you never got to know. It is also about the death of dreams, ambitions, hope for the future.

The aftercare, or lack of it, that we received after the second loss sent Samantha into a deep depression and she had to be admitted to a clinic.

I was devoid of hope and I felt as alone as you can ever imagine.

We tried again and made it to 20 weeks, a stage by which expectant parents usually feel optimistic. But Samantha got pre-eclampsia and we lost another baby.

The only way to treat pre-eclampsia is to deliver the baby. To see Samantha having to go through the pain of childbirth, knowing that our baby was already dead, was unbearable.

Medically, the way the hospital looked after Samantha was better than I could have hoped for. But, as a man, I felt in the way. When the doctors looked at me, it felt like they were asking: "What are you doing here?"

The feeling I had at the time was that the medical staff had no time or view on how to deal with the grieving father.

The next time we made it to 25 weeks before Samantha's high blood pressure returned. We had an emergency caesarean and gave birth to a baby girl. Claudia weighed just 428 grams. The hospital was sceptical that she would make it through the night. She proved us all wrong and lived in the neo-natal intensive care unit for 6 weeks.

Again, all hope of a future evaporated on the death of baby number four. What do you believe in? What can you believe in? I had lost all hope and optimism for a future.

By the time we suffered the next early miscarriage, we

knew the routine at the hospital and any feelings were numbed.

The most important thing in my life is the wellbeing of my wife and there was nothing I could do to make things better. I felt helpless. There were times when I thought why on earth have I made my wife pregnant? An overwhelming sense of guilt of putting her through all this when all I was worried about was loosing my hope.

I did not know how I was ever expected to "get over " seeing my wife so distressed, then burying our daughters, trying to deal with my own emotions while putting on the brave face to support my wife.

How do you deal with the in-laws? It was my fault that their precious child, their daughter was in such a distraught state. That is what I believed they thought.

I do not want to be negative about hospital staff because they looked after Samantha well. The support for fathers should come from elsewhere, not the midwives. Hospital managers do not seem to entertain the idea that care extends beyond the patient and to the wellbeing of the family.

When we consider the time pressures on the medical professionals, when is there time available for us? When we lost our premature baby we were offered the services of a counsellor. But this is not something I felt comfortable with.

We learned about a research unit at St. Thomas's, in London, that might be able to help us. Samantha was diagnosed with Antiphospholipid Syndrome (APS), a disorder that makes the blood clot because it has become too sticky and cannot squeeze through the tiny vessels in the placenta. It can also push up a pregnant woman's blood pressure. But medical guidelines deter testing for APS until there have been at least three miscarriages.

I wanted to leave and get away. There just seemed too many memories everywhere I went. I met an old friend who worked for BNP Paribas in Frankfurt and we talked about a job in Paris. Before long I relocated from London to Paris where I have been for just over a year.

As soon as the job was secured Samantha was pregnant again. We stuck with our plans to move but Samantha stayed on in the UK for treatment with me pounding the motorway from Paris to Orpington, in Kent, every weekend.

On July 17 2001, at 37 weeks, Ethan arrived.

The joy of seeing my son, his first breath, the opening of his eyes, his first move reaching out to me, means more to me than anything I can ever imagine - the hopes I have for him; an overwhelming all-consuming sense of protection; the sense of absolute and overwhelming love; the perfect and innocent form of a new born child and the beauty and miracle of life.

After all the heartache, I am privileged to experience these feelings, a healthy baby I can call my son. I look at him today, 15 months old and he is calling me daddy - something I never thought I would hear.

What more can I possibly ever ask for?

All three of us are enjoying life to the maximum in Paris.

Ethan Kunz is special. He's chirpy, curious and thrives on attention. He is our final salvation.

He has given us a future.

Martin Kunz
Head of Global Custody Product Development for BNP
Paribas Securities Services
Paris France

The drugs don't work

The gynaecologist sits behind his desk
Studying charts of numerous cycles
LH surges, follicle sizes
Missing eggs in the black hole of Calcutta
Weighing up slowly how to couch his words...
"The drugs don't work," he eventually says.
I smile and hum The Verve -
The joke's lost on him
It would be, wouldn't it.
Injections every other day
LH kits and killer stress
Waiting for a surge that never comes
Waiting for the chance to hatch an egg
And I try not to put pressure on the one I love
"The drugs don't work", we chew it over -
We know what it means.
"You've no chance".
He offers some Profasi
Kamikaze - what the hell
But the drugs don't work
So we're giving it up
Praying for luck
Low ovarian reserves, he says
Like they're gold in a vault
Nobody's fault.

Andrew Don

Tom's story

At 9.30pm, Sunday December 8 1991, our baby Janine was stillborn.

We do not know why she was born dead. It happens to some people and this time it was us.

Mary's pregnancy had been normal with no apparent problems. She, reluctantly, was going to have a normal birth - a "trial of scar" it was called. Mary prefers caesareans - less pain she reckons and more predictable.

On Sunday night as we were preparing to take Mary into hospital, she went into labour, with intense contractions about two minutes apart. We rushed her in and took the decision to perform a caesarean because the baby was distressed, and there was merconian (faecal matter from the baby which is dangerous if inhaled) in the amniotic fluid.

After Janine was born dead, one of the nurses came to me as I sat on the floor in the corner and said she had also lost a child and knew how I felt. I had not spoken to anyone who had lost a child before and her simple comments meant a lot.

We had the undivided attention of one nurse per shift over the next few days and had a large room, the hospital's home birth suite, to ourselves. The nurses would come in and sit and cry with us. Janine was with us when we wanted her to be. We had the photos, the clip of hair, the hand and footprints, the SANDS leaflets.

Teardrop stickers were placed on our door. As I would walk out of the room, groups of nurses would dissipate from their session of swapping stories of what had happened to us. I was acutely aware this was a serious thing that everyone took to heart - I felt cared for and supported; lost, confused and sad, but not lonely.

My heart wrenched when I would walk past one of the rooms and hear a baby's first cry - I wished I could have heard my own daughter's first cry. How I wished.

We had a few visitors, but many, many kind thoughts, messages and flowers. Some of our friends could look at Janine and even hold her. Some could not bear to look. That was okay by us. We understood.

I knew the babies I could hear who were born alive were not mine. It hurt hearing them cry. What was important was that we were still in the familiar surroundings of the labour ward with staff who had been through the pain of it with us. If we had gone to the post-natal ward, we might have had more difficulty coping with staff and other patients who did not know us.

It was important for our first son Gerry who had just turned two, a caring and sensitive child who figured out something was wrong, to be fully involved. Every adult he saw was crying. Naturally he figured out something bad had happened.

Over the years we have tried to keep the memory of Janine alive for him, by including her in our conversations, by remembering her birthday, by placing flowers on her memorial in the cemetery. He talks about her at his school with his friends who accept it without problems. It is the adults who have problems.

One of the most striking things about life after Janine is the smaller circle of friends we have and how our contacts now include many other bereaved parents. We realise how for many of our friends, it was too painful for them to talk to us. Reflecting four years later, we accept some of these friendships were just floating along anyway and we were not particularly close to them. What the loss of Janine did was to show us who our close friends were.

Losing a child is tough on everyone. No one wins, no one knows what to do or say. Some people do not know what to say so they say stupid things, or religious things. If you cannot think of saying something supportive, it is okay to not say anything. We appreciated those whose only words were: "I'm so sorry, I don't know what to say." That's fine, we did not know what to say either, but at least it acknowledged the pain, the loss of Janine and let us talk if we wanted to.

And talk we did. After a few months though, we were getting wise to what we said to people. Close people got the truth; pushy people got pushed away with half-truths.

Once, when I returned to work, a colleague who I was not particularly close to got me into her office on the first day back and grilled me about what had happened, wanting to know what we were "going to do about it", such as suing for damages. This was insensitive and uncalled for.

First, she invaded my grief as someone who was not close to me. She asked personal questions she had no right to ask. She did it on the first day back at work, showing no sensitivity at all. She made no effort to find out my feelings on the matter in terms of responsibility and blame and then imposed her own view on a situation she knew nothing about.

The reaction of my own parents, my mother especially, was particularly hard to deal with. Mum was devastated. She wanted to share her feelings and be supportive of us. We had never had a feelings-based relationship and it was foreign and new for this to be demanded of us. I told her I recognised she was really upset by the loss of Janine and so were we and that she was looking for support, but we could not give that to her. She needed to find that somewhere else, I said.

She got the message and we were free again to be together in our grief and not have to support anyone else. I am not sure what my mother did, but we still get on and it did not cause any new problems.

True friends stay around but other friends drop away. Friends do not know what to do, they do not know how to start conversations, whether to talk about the baby and how they will cope when you cry. They do not want to be the cause of you crying and they feel guilty when they avoid you.

We chose carefully whom we contacted and we were conscious that we had to set the scene and the tone of the contact. We would casually bring up Janine in the conversation. "We've not been out much since Janine was born, but would like to see you sometime."

We got many, many sympathy cards after Janine was born. Christmas came 13 days later but we got few Christmas cards. We wanted to be normal, we did not like being abnormal or special. We wanted to be boring and blend in to the background. We should have been getting Christmas cards.

There is no best way to handle this. Special events are always difficult for bereaved parents, reminding them of their loss. Janine's birth being so close to Christmas just made everything so much more unbearable.

It surprised us whom we got messages from. Some people we had met only briefly, or had some obscure contact with, sent us cards while we did not hear from others who knew us well. Every day more sympathy cards would arrive, some we recognised as having a special message. Those were from parents who had also lost babies, through stillbirth and miscarriage. Their messages gave us comfort, acknowledging that we were not alone.

Some messages of sympathy carried religious script. We had attended church, but were not deeply religious, although Mary's faith was stronger than mine. When you lose a child, you lose lots of other things as well, such as loss of innocence, your faith in the medical profession, your understanding of the rules of life - that bad things only happen to bad people, your faith in God and your religion. Why has God done this to us? Saying it was God's will does not help. Saying he has a spot in heaven for Janine does not help. Those thoughts are as unhelpful as saying you are young enough to try again. What we wanted was our girl. God does not make sense, God did not help, what use was he?

I was employed as a social worker in a large local government providing services to help old people living in their home as they became more frail. My manager's reaction to my loss helped me greatly in my return to work part-time about a month after Janine died. I did not return to full time work for about three months - I needed that space.

Our only child Gerry had to be hospitalised twice not long after with severe stomach pain, vomiting and diarrhoea.

It was first diagnosed as gastro-enteritis, but when a second episode resulted in him being sent to emergency surgery they found he had a 'second appendix' or Meckles Diverticulum. which twisted his bowel and constricted it. They removed the Meckles and his appendix and he's been fine since.

Mary was trying to get pregnant while all this was going on but got a virus called CMV (Cito meglio virus), which results in deformities or miscarriage if pregnant. So that meant Mary could not get pregnant while the virus was active.

1992 was a horrible year, an emotional roller coaster.

Mary was eventually clear of the virus and became pregnant. We planned a caesarean on October 16th 1993, about two weeks before the due date. We used the same team of doctors as we used with Janine. We even asked for one of "our" midwives that had been with us after Janine's birth to be with us.

We needed people who knew us, knew our history, and who were going to be supportive and understand if we went a bit loopy in the process.

I knew I was nervous about the impending birth of Travis - we knew he was a boy. We did not want any surprises during birth this time - but did not realise quite how stressed I was until I saw the first photos taken after his birth.

I looked like I had appeared when Janine was born - drawn, shocked, and unhappy. I had also not realised until Travis's first sounds, that I'd been waiting two years to hear my baby's first cry.

The joy that should be associated with a healthy contented new baby came slowly, but was tinged with sadness and fears about getting too close. I was afraid he would always miss out on things I had done for Gerry.

For instance, I had written a detailed diary of my feelings from the time we knew Mary was pregnant with Gerry right up until the birth of Janine when Gerry was two. Now I have stopped recording those things and Travis will miss out as he grows up.

Older siblings are affected in ways we least expect. Gerry was sad when Janine was born and we have kept his memories alive by talking about her and regularly taking him to place flowers on her memorial at the cemetery.

During Mary's pregnancy with Travis, he saw a baby being

born on TV. He said: "The baby's born, now it's dead and people will cry." His response took us aback. We gently introduced him to new healthy babies we knew and also revisited the hospital nursery to show him how most babies survived. When Travis arrived safely, he loved his new brother very much, and it was wonderful to see; but always the "What if" questions are there and remain unanswered.

We wanted to keep trying to have another girl, and Mary became pregnant in September 1994. The new baby was due when Travis was about 18 months old. Mary had a miscarriage at 12 weeks.

The ultrasound showed an empty placenta; there never had been a baby. It was called a blighted ovum, and is caused when conception occurs, but the cells stop dividing successfully at an early stage. Losing that pregnancy was hard, but not as hard as losing Janine. The fact that there was no baby, no heartbeat, made it a lot easier for me. What we lost was more the expectation and the happiness that Mary was pregnant. It took time to get over that, and to resurrect our self-esteem to try again.

When Janine died, we wanted to just keep on having children, not wanting to miss out on any opportunity after seeing how precious they are and how quickly things can go from hope to tragedy.

Having another child after losing Janine helped the healing and restored a little of our faith in ourselves, the medical profession, God and our true friends. But it is not without its own traumas and should not be entertained lightly by others who have lost a child. It does help to soften the memories, but nothing should be done to try to erase those memories. Learn to live with them and they will become less raw over time. But never try to forget the child you've lost.

Experiencing this loss has made me more empathetic with the people I am trying to help and I am a better helper. I would rather have my daughter, but there have been positive things to have happened as a result of her death.

I have become more focused in my work, in balancing home and family and in what I want to get out of life. I was able to leave the security of permanent work and do contract and locum consultancy, which is somewhat unusual in my industry. I did it because I wanted to refocus my life, to be more flexible.

Through the death of Janine I discovered more meaning to life.

On April 11th 1996 Mary gave birth to a girl and we named her Cassandra. She was born by caesarean 14 days early.

My tears started as the operation started and did not stop until well after she was born alive and we knew all was okay. I did not want to be there because I feared another stillbirth. I buried my head in the pillow beside Mary and just sobbed. When the doctors lifted her out and showed us over the top of the sheets, I only glanced and did not believe what I was seeing. I was still expecting the worst.

With the slow realisation of her life, her uniqueness, her beauty, I felt a great load slowly lifting - life had something to offer again.

Tom
Western Australia.
(Tom and all the names in Tom's story
have been changed at the request of the writer)

Before the first meeting with my daughters - June 2000

My daughters to be
As I sit and write
You do not know me
I'm some hypothetical;
A knot of anxiety in your tummies.
You fear -
I fear too
For the pain you've both suffered
For the lives you've been through.
Already I feel I've failed you.
But I want to succeed
To give you back your childhood
To see you laugh and smile
Reconcile the pain
And let your souls free

This is from the heart
I love you - even now
Before we've even started
And I pray you will let me in
Accept my love.

So hard it is to trust for you
I know it well - I've been there, too

Andrew Don

Useful UK Contacts

ARC (Antenatal Results & Choices)
Provides support and information to parents throughout the antenatal testing process.
Web: www.arc-uk.org - Helpline: 020 7631 0285

Babyloss, a voluntary organisation
An online resource available to anyone affected by the loss of a baby during pregnancy, at birth or shortly afterwards.
Web: www.babyloss.com

Baby Mailing Preference Service
Designed to help reduce the number of baby-related mailings following the death of a baby.
Web: www.mpsonline.org.uk/bmpsr - Tel: 020 7291 3310

Compassionate Friends
An organisation of bereaved parents and their families offering understanding, support and encouragement to others after the death of a child or children.
Web: www.tcf.org.uk - Helpline: 08451 23 23 04

Cruse Bereavement Care
Exists to promote the well-being of bereaved people and to enable anyone bereaved by death to understand their grief and cope with their loss.
Web: www.crusebereavementcare.org.uk - Helpline: 0870 167 1677

The Ectopic Pregnancy Trust
Provides support and information to couples who have suffered an ectopic pregnancy.
Web: www.ectopic.org - Helpline: 01895 238 025

Foundation for the Study of Infant Deaths
Works to prevent unexpected infant deaths, promotes baby health and offers support to bereaved families.
Web: www.sids.org.uk - Helpline: 0870 787 0554

The Miscarriage Association
Provides support and information to those suffering the
effects of pregnancy loss
Web: www.miscarriageassociation.org.uk - Helpline: 01924 200799

Useful International Contacts

Sudden Infant Death Syndrome and Other Infant Death
A charitable, not-for-profit voluntary agency for those who have
experienced Sudden Infant Death Syndrome or other infant death.
Web: www.sids-network.org

The National Stillbirth Society
A US organisation set up by Richard Olsen, whose story is included
in this book, to "educate and agitate" for greater stillbirth awareness,
research and reform.
Web: www.stillnomore.org

The Compassionate Friends Worldwide
US - www.compassionatefriends.org
Canada - www.tcfcanada.net
Netherlands - www.vook.nl
Belgium - www.ovok.be
Austrailia - www.angelfire.com/id/tcfbrisbane

SANDS Australia
Promoting awareness, knowledge, support and understanding
following the death of a baby from the time of conception through
to infancy.
Web: www.sands.org.au

September 2004

Lara Jean
I miss you still
I always will

But life is good now
Life is good
No guilt
No shame

And that's okay
That's okay.

Andrew Don

Glossary

Amniocentesis – a test for genetic disorders in the foetus. Down's syndrome can be diagnosed early in pregnancy with this procedure at about 15-16 weeks.

Amniotic fluid – a watery fluid that surrounds the foetus throughout pregnancy. Too much or too little is associated with abnormalities and complications.

Antiphospholipid Syndrome (APS) - the name given to a disease which involves the immune system The manifestations of APS are variable. It is associated with recurring miscarriage in early pregnancy, loss of a baby after the first trimester (13 weeks), pre-eclampsia in pregnancy and unexpectedly small babies

Apnoea – a temporary cessation of breathing which occurs in some newborn babies.

Blighted ovum -. an egg is fertilized and attaches itself to the uterine wall, but the embryo doesn't develop further. Results in miscarriage

Braxton Hicks - Intermittent contractions of the uterus increasing in frequency as pregnancy nears completion.

Caesarean – delivery of a baby through an incision in the abdomen and uterus through which the baby is removed.

Chlamydia – Chlamydia trachomatis is a bacterium which causes a sexually-transmitted infection.

Down's Syndrome – a birth defect in which the affected person has an extra chromosome 21, making 47 in all. This results in a disruption to the growth of the developing baby. There are three different types of this affliction.

Ectopic pregnancy- when the baby develops outside the womb

In-vitro fertilisation (IVF) - fertilisation outside the body in a test tube

Pre-eclampsia - a condition characterised by high blood pressure, persistent excessive swelling of the hands, feet and ankles and sometimes the face, and large amounts of protein in the urine. The only way to alleviate it is by giving birth and often the baby will have to be induced early. Pre-eclampsia, if not managed, can lead to eclampsia where a seizure occurs. The patient will be at serious risk of a stroke.

Profasi - (human chorionic gonadotropin) is given to induce ovulation and the actual release of mature eggs from the ovaries of women following treatment with follicle stimulating hormone.

Sudden Infant Death Syndrome (SIDS) - the abrupt and unexpected death of a baby that appeared to be perfectly healthy. Often the baby's parents will have put their child to bed at night only to discover the next morning that it has mysteriously died.

SANDS

28 Portland Place,
London, W1B 1LY
Helpline: 020 7436 5881
Office: 020 7436 7940
Fax: 020 7436 3715
Email: support@uk-sands.org
Website: www.uk-sands.org

In the UK, 17 babies a day are stillborn or die within the first twenty eight days of life; a devastating bereavement for the parents and for their families and friends.

SANDS is a national organisation which was established by bereaved parents in 1978 and registered as a charity in 1981.

Today, SANDS supports over 4,000 parents every year, and works with health and social care professionals to improve the quality of services provided to bereaved families. SANDS also promotes research into the causes of stillbirths and neonatal deaths and changes in practice that could save more babies' lives.

The key services that SANDS provides, include:

National Helpline

Anyone affected by the death of a baby, whether a bereaved parent, family member, health or social care professional can talk in confidence to an experienced support worker.

Local Groups run by and for bereaved parents

SANDS currently has a large network of local support Groups and individual contacts in the UK, plus a growing number of overseas Groups. Together they offer a range of services which include bereavement support, memorial services, liaison with local hospitals, and fundraising for facilities such as a special room within a hospital or a SANDS garden.

Information and Publications

SANDS support leaflets focus on the many emotional and practical issues which bereaved families face. SANDS "Guidelines for Health Professionals" has been the foundation for many improvements in bereavement care.

Many parents find comfort in reading others parents' stories of their baby's death, and our website, quarterly newsletter and a growing number of new books such as *"Fathers Feel too"* reflect the experience of bereavement from many perspectives.